Pick your battles wisely. Especially the ones within you.

OFF THE BEATEN PATH:

LISA GROVES

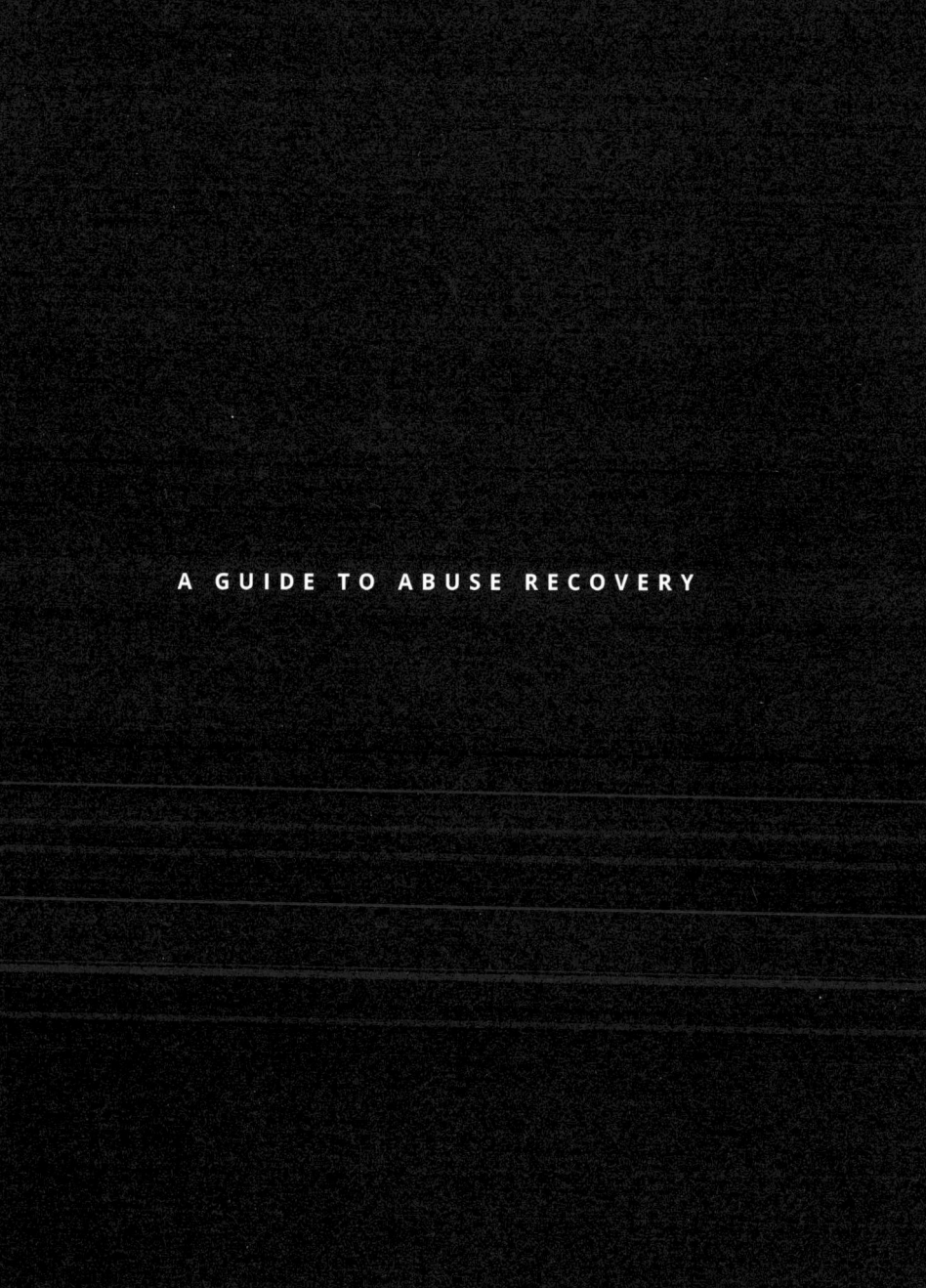
A GUIDE TO ABUSE RECOVERY

Copyright © 2016 by Lisa Groves. All Rights Reserved.

No part of this book may be transmitted, reproduced or otherwise used in any manner whatsoever without the written permission of the publisher except brief quotations included in critical articles and reviews.

The author of this book does not dispense medical advice or prescribe the use of any technique as a form of treatment for any physical or psychological condition. The author is not a healthcare provider and this book shall not be used to replace professional medical advice. The intent of the author is solely to offer information of a general nature for educational and entertainment purposes. This book includes the author's recollection of certain events, related to the best of the author's knowledge. Some identities have been changed or are composites. The author and the publisher assume no responsibility and hereby disclaim any liability resulting directly or indirectly from the use of this book.

Inquiries to: www.lisagroves.com

First edition: 2016
Printed in the United States

10 9 8 7 6 5 4 3 2 1

Library of Congress Control Number: 2015908349

ISBN: 978-0-578-16005-4

Published by I've Been Meaning To Write LLC
Scottsdale, Arizona

DEDICATION
////////////////////////////

"I love watching my husband age. Knowing that as the way of time has changed the boy I married into the refined creature before me, so too has it shaped and reshaped all that I am, and this man has remained a loyal witness to it all."

for Paul

CONTENTS

Prologue		XIII
The punch list		17
The abuser		19
The epiphany		21

Step one: safety

1	What is the last thing you did out of fear?	25
2	What is the last thing you did for too long?	33

Step two: trust

3	What is the last thing you overanalyzed?	41
4	When is the last time you ignored your intuition?	49
5	When is the last time you hesitated?	57

Step three: power

6	Where is the last place you were trapped?	63
7	What is the last thing you tried to force?	73
8	When is the last time you overreacted?	79

Step four: self-esteem

9	When is the last time you were bullied?	87
10	What is the last thing you tried to fake?	95
11	What is the last thing you took personally?	101

Step five: intimacy

12	What is the last thing you ran away from?	109
13	When is the last time you gave too much?	117

Epilogue	121
About the author	123
Notes	125

[PROLOGUE]

I can still see the shape of each bead as they rattled on the wall beside me. Mother Mary, perfectly coiffed, her stoic face carved deep into ivory. Yes there we dangled, side by side, that colossal rosary and me. Determined hands around my throat, easily pinning me up high like a reminder to buy milk on Tuesday.

It was the day I died, the day I hung there on that filthy bedroom wall. I closed my eyes, dropped my head, and wondered if Mother Mary minded.

Twenty years later.

It was the most important note I would ever write - at least that much was certain - and to connect with this truth was like parting with *bone*.

My desk was cool to the touch, but my mind, my mind was on *fire*. I think of my daughter, her words to me like tiny gold threads animating everything once lifeless within me. I took a deep breath in and smiled softly. Soon sticks and stones would bury all of my bones, but her words had never hurt me.

And then I think of that wall, just Mother Mary and me. Both of us defined by a family we had not freely chosen and that was not of our own design.

I twirled the bottles in my hands, nervously humming now. I think of my husband, his hot breath above me, laboring so mightily to be my cure. His mouth moving to mine in the darkness, whispering "you are just the *bomb*."   *(cont.)*

Such an interesting irony I think sharply, holding the bottles up to the light now. This sweet man, he'll never know how well he *knows* me. Yes treacherous but buried deep, I am an obsolete minefield. A battleground beyond its time. Still capable of sabotage, but ultimately irrelevant.

Sometimes I'll be sitting in yoga with my hands in prayer or squeezing a peach at the market or absently stroking my daughter's hair and I can still feel those hands, ringing out my voice like the ducks that hang in the windows of China Town.

I closed my eyes and nodded slowly. The sun was gone and I was ready to write now. The note. *My Suicide Note*. I chose a pen, of course. These were not the sort of words you could change or take back.

And then there in the dark I laid them all out, the acts of my final *undoing*. The belts and the welts and the bruises to hide and the way strands of my hair would fly through the air and stick to the blood on my face as I tried to run but there was nowhere to hide and I *never* won.

Still I kept running. Until that day on the wall. The day I died to that kind of inevitable defeat that cramps and burns through your chest, like a night of cigarettes, or swimming too soon after lunch.

And so the note. *My Suicide Note*. I leaned in farther and studied it closely. And when I looked away, I knew just what to do.

I would start with a list. The *Punch List*.

THINGS THAT ARE BEATEN INTO YOU

THE PUNCH LIST

1 Avoidance

2 Repeating the past

3 Fear of trusting other people

4 Fear of trusting yourself

5 Fear of taking risks

6 Powerlessness

7 Fear of losing control

8 Defensiveness

9 Fear that you are a bad person

10 Fear that you do not belong

11 Self-blame

12 Fear of commitment

13 Fear that you are unloveable

1 THEY DENY

2 THEY MINIMIZE

3 THEY BLAME THEIR VICTIMS

THE ABUSER

Abusers are not complicated. They are not clever. They are not even *interesting*, as evil people can sometimes be. Abusers are rote. They are predictable. They are boring.

It never happened. You are exaggerating. You are mentally ill.

It wasn't that bad. I barely touched you. You are overreacting.

You provoked me. You had it coming. You left me no choice.

Do not waste your life searching for the reason an abuser abused you. It is the same reason a dog licks its balls: because it *can*. Yes you - as you - are irrelevant. You could be anyone. In the mind of an abuser, *you* do not matter at all.

★ THE EPIPHANY ★

You are not what has been *done to* you.

We all use one another to learn the lessons that brought us here.

It is inevitable.

It is in fact the *genesis of all attraction*.

The question is not whether you will use and be used.

The question is whether you *learn*.

STEP ONE: SAFETY

AVOIDANCE

1 WHAT IS THE LAST THING YOU DID OUT OF FEAR?

INVOLUNTARY INTOXICATION (LEGAL DEF.) A chemical intoxication by design, fraud, or artifice without any fault on the part of the intoxicated person and which results in diminished capacity.

[DEFINITION]

HYPERAROUSAL

In response to imminent threat, a chain of rapidly occurring chemical reactions mobilize your body's resources to prepare for defensive action. Known as *arousal*, your nervous system stimulates your adrenal glands, momentarily heightening your senses and accelerating your heart and lung function. Arousal is a normal, adaptive survival response.

*Hyper*arousal is a condition in which your body remains in a continuous state of arousal, reacting as though it were under a present threat even in benign situations. At the root of avoidance, Hyperarousal drives you to make decisions that are not based in fact but in *fear*.

In a state of low arousal, a person will choose the more pleasant of two alternatives. Because unfamiliar stimuli increase arousal, however, a person who is already *Hyper*aroused will avoid novelty and choose familiar behavior, even if offered a less painful alternative.

When exposed to prolonged or random acts of violence, abuse victims become Hyperaroused as a primitive form of self-preservation. Now necessary to their feelings of security, these victims may remain Hyperaroused indefinitely, even long after their exposure to violence has ended.

A maladaptive chemical response of the brain, Hyperarousal effectively "drugs" abuse victims into a chronic state of fear.

To overcome fear, you must first decide that you want to know the truth more than you want to feel secure.

Security is like a wickedly skilled lover.

But truth, truth is the reason you *come*.

"Do not wait for some magical moment to fall down on you like fairy dust and free you from what is. Letting go does not *happen* to you. Letting go is a decision. It is a choice, like the choice to hold on that you made just before it. Letting go is - in the end and *always* - a deliberate act of will."

REPEATING

2   WHAT IS THE LAST THING YOU DID FOR TOO LONG?

THE PAST

COMPULSIVE

REENACTMENT

A complex psychological phenomenon, Compulsive Reenactment is the subconscious urge to recreate abuse experiences from your past in an effort to resolve childhood trauma.

Believing you are somehow *broken*, you find yourself inexplicably drawn to people who exhibit the very same character traits and behaviors that you observed in your abuser.

Genuinely unaware of your own true motivation, you use these people as unwitting "surrogates" for your abuser. The stage now set, you are able to reenact abuse scenarios from your past, reprocessing them and changing their dynamics until you finally feel a sense of resolution.

Compulsive Reenactment is a result of the inherent tension between the desire to disassociate yourself from the abuse you experienced and the *simultaneous* desire to purge the trauma associated with that abuse by reenacting it.

Despite its pathological nature, Compulsive Reenactment is not an attempt to harm yourself but rather a misguided attempt to *heal* yourself. A deep, insidious pattern, driving you to create what are simply new *versions* of the same abusive relationship.

Over and over and over again, you *return to the scene of the crime.*

[DEFINITION]

There can be no rebirth without a death before it. This is the price of liberation - which frees you - but which is not free. You must be willing to walk away from every relationship, life circumstance, or fundamental belief system you have ever created, observed, or relied upon.

And then you must burn your bridges.

I know, it is a brutal paradox. That you only find a new life by burning one down. Letting all that has been fly up into your face and then slowly dissolve there, like useless road salt just before spring. But it does not matter how many failures may define you or lie right behind you.

The very definition of the word "life" is the capacity to *change*.

STEP TWO: TRUST

FEAR OF TRUSTING

3   WHAT IS THE LAST THING YOU OVERANALYZED?

OTHER PEOPLE

"If what we think we become, I am in deep shit."

MISTRUST

As a child, you learned complex emotional concepts like "trust" by grouping your experiences into crude extremes. Something was either good or bad, black or white. Your initial understanding of trust was very concrete because you lacked the maturity to differentiate the behavior of one trusted person from that of another trusted person.

If a trusted person *abused* you, abuse simply became part of your understanding of a "trusting relationship".

Viewing the world through this paradigm, it is impossible to discern who is in fact trustworthy. Everyone around you is a potential threat, especially the people who are the closest to you. Unable to trust organically, you feel driven to constantly analyze all of your relationships, plagued by nagging doubts and a deep sense of *suspicion*.

[DEFINITION]

In order to trust you must first accept that no one is completely trustworthy.

Everyone you love has the potential to betray you, large or small, leaving you to plod through the remnants of idolization that disappoint and then darken, like dirty snow.

No one is completely trustworthy.

Now, you just need to let go.

FEAR OF TRUSTING

4   WHEN IS THE LAST TIME YOU IGNORED YOUR INTUITION?

YOURSELF

"Intuition is not a thought. Intuition is what happens *in between* your thoughts. It is your direct perception of truth, without any reasoning process."

GASLIGHTING

A covert act of psychological warfare, Gaslighting is a tactic in which an abuser presents false information to a victim in order to manipulate the victim into doubting their own intuition, perceptions and memories.

The term comes from the 1938 play, *Gas Light*, where a husband attempts to drive his wife insane by dimming the gas-powered lights in their home and then denying that the lights changed when his wife points it out.

Using a pattern of deliberate deception, Gaslighting conditions a victim to automatically believe their abuser's version of events and then question the realness of their own experiences.

An extremely effective form of psychological abuse, Gaslighting quietly dismantles a victim's sense of intuition, and with it, their sense of self-trust.

[DEFINITION]

You are born trusting yourself. The manifestation of intuition, self-trust is the force by which you observe, discern, and take action in the world around you.

While self-confidence is in your mind - cerebral and calculated - self-trust is in your guts and your *bones*.

When you have been abused, trusting yourself again is not so much a doing as an *un*doing. A *fearless* rebirth. It is making a conscious return to your natural state, listening to your own intuition at the deepest level.

"If you want to feel secure, learn to fall madly in love with change. It is, in the end, the only thing that will never leave you."

FEAR OF

5   WHEN IS THE LAST TIME YOU HESITATED?

TAKING RISKS

So I'm at the library and find an old Black's law dictionary for sale. It was from the 1940's and the inside cover was inscribed with the words *Georgetown Law School*, followed by a row of men's names, each one crossed out with pen by his successor.

No matter how important we may believe ourselves to be, eventually we will all be crossed off of the Great List.

Do what you need to do, and do it now.

STEP THREE: POWER

POWERLESSNESS

6   WHERE IS THE LAST PLACE YOU WERE TRAPPED?

LEARNED

HELPLESSNESS

If you are trapped in an uncontrollable situation, repeatedly overpowered or outwitted by an abuser, your mind will eventually "give up". Resigned to your existing circumstances, you will stop looking for opportunities to fight back or flee.

A *crippling* psychological force, Learned Helplessness has trapped you in a chronic cycle of powerlessness. A slave to its inertia, you may remain in this state forever, the feeling of powerlessness expanding to every aspect of your life and relationships.

Even when you are given the opportunity to assert yourself you likely will not act on it. You have "learned that you are helpless", that no matter what action you take, you will never have the power necessary to escape an abusive situation.

[DEFINITION]

"Like a bad roommate, powerlessness doesn't really *do* anything. It's like the scab your mother warned you not to pick. It just sits there, reminding you that you are not healed."

FLIGHT, FIGHT OR

FREEZE

The manifestation of arousal, Flight or Fight is a physiological reaction that prepares your body to flee or fight perceived danger. Hardwired into your brain as genetic wisdom, it is designed to protect your body from harm. But when you do not have time for flight or the strength to fight, your brain will release chemicals that cause you to *freeze,* like a mouse playing dead when caught by a cat.

A primitive mechanism of defense, the Freeze Response enables you to detach from fear and pain in order to better endure your circumstances. While Flight or Fight is about having hope - the confidence you can outrun or outfight your attacker - the *Freeze* Response is about losing hope.

Because they are inherently vulnerable, children who experience ongoing trauma become habituated to freezing when confronted by danger. The victims of child abuse often harbor deep anger toward themselves for not doing more to fight back or flee, leaving them prone to feel "frozen" and powerless as adults.

[DEFINITION]

Forgive everyone.

Until you forgive, the very same people you blame for your misery will forever be your keepers.

Forgiveness is your way out.

It is a sovereign act of self-preservation. It is not weakness. It is the opposite of weakness.

Forgiveness has balls and bones and the stones to rebuild you.

FEAR OF

7   WHAT IS THE LAST THING YOU TRIED TO FORCE?

LOSING CONTROL

OBSESSIVE-COMPU

LSIVE DISORDER

Human beings need order. They need a framework that can account for their experiences. When an abuser randomly alternates between affection and violence, it undermines their victim's fundamental ability to view the world as a place that is orderly and just.

At its very core, abuse shatters the mind's sense of *control*.

A debilitating combination of intrusive thoughts (obsessions) and repetitive behaviors (compulsions), *Obsessive-Compulsive Disorder* is a direct response to this chaos.

Victims of abuse often enter a frightening psychological free fall, driven by overwhelming fears and anxieties. Desperate to once again feel secure, they become obsessed with rules and details. Over time, these obsessions morph into *compulsions*, where victims repeat strict rituals in an effort to ground themselves and create "structure" by using arbitrary order.

[DEFINITION]

GRAVE CONCERNS

Sixty-seven days ago I discovered the utility of making major life decisions in a cemetery.

Ripe ground for an epiphany, indeed.

Surrounded by people crammed into boxes, I rapped on the walls of my *own*. Rigid little boxes, housing all I hold dear - my *empire* - lined up neatly like the soup cans in my grandmother's pantry.

Until sixty-seven days ago, that is.

I suppose it doesn't really matter what particular transaction drove me to seek clarity on a wet and dirty path separating rows of people I've never even met. The big stuff usually falls under love, money, sex or family, so take your pick.

But as for my epiphany? Here is the skinny. Control is always, invariably, *ultimately* just an *illusion*.

When my gal-pals ask me for the fast track to an epiphany of their own, here is what I've got to say: while I was busily straightening boxes, a good force descended and shook me awake. Then left me lying *in* its wake.

Like a bloody nose that comes in the night.

There are only three things in this world I know for certain. One, *nothing* in this world is certain. Two, nice girls nurture but do not possess. And Three, if you sit in a graveyard surrounded by plots, you will learn how to live, outside of the box.

"Surround yourself with people who believe you are a better person than you actually *are*. They will eventually bring out the best in you."

DEFENSIVENESS

8   WHEN IS THE LAST TIME YOU OVERREACTED?

HYPERVIGILANCE

A dramatically heightened state of awareness, Hypervigilance is the experience of being constantly "on guard", highly suspicious of the people around you and watching them closely for signs of threat.

In response to unavoidable danger, victims of abuse become Hypervigilant as a way to manage their state of vulnerability. They unknowingly study patterns of behavior, and then use those observations to anticipate when abuse is most likely to occur.

An involuntary, subconscious reflex, Hypervigilance is a result of the innate drive toward self-preservation. It is a tool of *survival*, leaving abuse victims prone to perceive threats and react defensively, even in non-threatening situations.

[DEFINITION]

Pick your battles wisely. Especially the ones within you.

STEP FOUR: SELF-ESTEEM

"Like a rape of the *mind*, abuse calls into question your most basic assumptions about the *self* as capable and inherently worthy."

FEAR THAT YOU

9   WHEN IS THE LAST TIME YOU WERE BULLIED?

ARE A BAD PERSON

Fruit of the Poisonous Tree (legal def.) The doctrine that evidence spawned by illegal government activity is fundamentally flawed due to its original taint. Because the "tree" or origin is judged poisonous, any "fruit" that it bears will inevitably be tainted.

UNPICKED

It was the heaviest thing I had ever lifted, its thick metal legs sunk deep into dirty linoleum as I dragged it toward the phone. But I was nine and outweighed and too late to save her, watching ancient curtains sway as he beat her to the floor. Me climbing up on that heavy chair and her birdlike arms flapping the air, a sad duo of futile resistance.

I closed my eyes as he stood over her, triumphant. Yes they were my *roots*, and to suddenly meet with this realization made my tiny tongue feel thick and hot and useless.

And then the police, cold and blue. Looking down at me with a tired mix of pity and impatience. Their eyes dark but knowing. Yes I was so small but they could still see that *I am* the fruit of the poisonous tree.

The biggest barrier to happiness - at least as I see it - is absorbing someone else's impression of you.

It is unreliable. It is limited to their experience of you, which is limited by human agenda - both yours and their own.

You are good enough for happiness.

Now, get on with your life.

Squatter's Rights (legal def.)   A method of gaining title to real property through the open, continuous, and adverse possession of it to the exclusion of its true owner for a period of time prescribed by law.

FEAR THAT YOU

10   WHAT IS THE LAST THING YOU TRIED TO FAKE?

DO NOT BELONG

"You can measure the entire arch of your psychological and spiritual evolution by the way you respond to rejection. Rejection is a gift. A valuable opportunity to refine, or even *define* yourself. Lately, the more I am rejected, the better I actually feel about myself. Not in the fa la la yogi Zen master kind of way. But in the solid, strong, *I finally know who I am* kind of way."

I spent years trying to assimilate into the normalcy around me. Crouched down low, I laid dubious roots. Just a clever girl with a bad pedigree and unclean hands.

I thought the passing of time could wall off the good and *true* me from what had been *done to* me - the way your body will grow bone around a foreign mass inside you.

Do not concern yourself with belonging. Your work is not to assimilate. You have likely already done that work. Your work now is to *leap*.

ND
SELF-BLAME

11   WHAT IS THE LAST THING YOU TOOK PERSONALLY?

CHARACTEROLOG

ICAL SELF-BLAME

The ultimate act of *self-incrimination*, Characterological Self-Blame is the propensity to blame your own personal character for the fact that you are being abused.

While *Behavioral Self-Blame* is the belief that your outward actions trigger abuse, Characterological Self-Blame is believing that your fundamental character - your very *nature* - is to blame.

Suddenly things make sense. Now there is a *reason* you are being abused. There is something inherently wrong with you and therefore you *deserve* to be abused.

Ironically, establishing this sort of causal relationship between your character and abuse can actually fool you into feeling a *stronger* sense of self-esteem and resilience. By blaming yourself for being abused, you are able to hold on to the belief that you have the power to *prevent* that abuse by "fixing" yourself and becoming worthy.

Your darkest psychological coping mechanism, Characterological Self-Blame allows your feelings of weakness and vulnerability to be replaced with the illusion of control.

[DEFINITION]

What other people do is not because of *you*.

Make this your mantra.

Say it over and over and over again, until you feel it on your skin and then deep in your bones.

It is the battleground of your repair.

In the end, the makings of freedom.

STEP FIVE: INTIMACY

"When your body can't flee abuse, your *mind* will. In an act of survival you build a psychological wall around yourself to prevent anyone from emotionally reaching you. Inside of this refuge you are able to feel secure, as only your *body* is being abused - the true *you* is now safe at a distance."

FEAR OF

12 WHAT IS THE LAST THING YOU RAN AWAY FROM?

COMMITMENT

[DEFINITION]

ATTACHMENT

We are all born into a natural state of dependence. Attachment is the deep connection formed between you and your caregivers in your first years of life. It is a fundamental human need, deeply rooted in evolution. Attachment is your very first instinct. It is also your most important one, because without Attachment you would not *survive*.

Innately powerful, your initial attachments set the template for all of your future relationships.

The base of your social foundation, Attachment teaches you the intimate dynamic between trust and devotion. When a caregiver becomes *abusive*, however, suddenly the very same person who has been your source of nurturance is now also a threat against which you need protection. Trapped in this paradox, you must maneuver to ensure a level of autonomy and distance is maintained between you and the people you are closest to.

Over time, the victims of abuse learn to equate their feelings of intimacy and attachment with the feeling of *fear*. Unwilling to accept this vulnerability, they quickly divest and "cut their losses", running away from any person or situation that threatens their sense of complete independence.

NOMAD

When I was six years old I deliberately dropped my brand-new baby doll down a dark and rotting well in my parents' backyard. It was the same year I made a lavender Christmas tree ornament with the sentiment "I like *alone*."

When I was *twenty*-six, an old, old friend smoking furiously and with unqualified command calmly informed me that it was impossible to love another person unconditionally. If such a love were possible, she reasoned, then we would love every person that we encountered and to the same degree.

I conceded her cold, calculating position - until I gave birth to the cure for *condition*.

Now we had decided to name her Madeline, but I knew right away she was Mad. Crying for roots and a home she would not leave me *alone* as I battled to love with the heart of a *no Mad*.

And yet, despite my fight, I lay quietly in bed and slowly take inventory. Now that I am approaching *thirty*-six, I know more, and therefore "I" no more.

Unconditional love defies reason, rhyme and requirement. It is unconcerned with the harvest. And yes, sometimes it even defies the *self*.

Recently, my buddy Nate laid it out like this: *(cont.)*

"Love - the kind given to one person over the course of a lifetime - is borne of the desire to believe in something greater than oneself."

What a mad, *Mad* notion.

FEAR THAT YOU

13   WHEN IS THE LAST TIME YOU GAVE TOO MUCH?

ARE UNLOVEABLE

Your job is not to become good enough. Your job is to accept that you already *are* good enough.

The earth muffins call this process self-love. The pragmatist in me calls it spiritual blue balls.

Either way, this is your true beginning.

[EPILOGUE]

So it's Saturday night and I'm doing my laundry and listening to the squeals of little girls as they run through my house playing hide-and-seek and my husband just kissed my forehead and called me his "beautiful bride" and I'm about as far off course as I've ever been and thinking that maybe I've been wrong this whole time - that maybe *this* is the grand adventure, after all.

I smoked a dozen or so cigarettes, lining up spent matches in battle formation, patiently waiting. Broken down, I was just fumbling in the dark, beating off my demons and trying to find god. This book came like a spiritual booty call.

I know, it's a little bit irreverent.

So sue me.

 lisagroves.com

 facebook.com/authorlisagroves

 twitter.com/abuse_recovery_

 instagram.com/authorlisagroves

LISA GROVES, JD IS A FORMER TRIAL LAWYER, A YOGA TEACHER, AND THE FOUNDER + PRESIDENT OF I'VE BEEN MEANING TO WRITE LLC, A BOUTIQUE MARKETING AND PUBLISHING FIRM.

SHE HOLDS A DOCTOR OF JURISPRUDENCE DEGREE, UNDERGRADUATE DEGREES IN JOURNALISM AND WOMEN'S STUDIES, AND A TEACHING CERTIFICATE IN YOGA PRACTICE AND PHILOSOPHY.

HERSELF A VICTIM OF PHYSICAL VIOLENCE, OFF THE BEATEN PATH: A GUIDE TO ABUSE RECOVERY © 2016 IS LISA'S MOST RECENT WORK OF NONFICTION AND JOURNEY THROUGH ABUSE RECOVERY.

LISA RESIDES IN SCOTTSDALE, ARIZONA WITH HER HUSBAND, PAUL BLOOMQUIST, MD AND DAUGHTER MADELINE MARY.

PHOTOGRAPH © MADELINE MARY BLOOMQUIST

NOTES

NOTES